Michael Jackson

The Man in the Mirror

By James McCarthy

ABSTRACT SOUNDS BOOKS LTD

Abstract Sounds Books Ltd
Unit 207, Buspace Studios, Conlan Street, London W10-5AP
www.abstractsoundsbooks.com

© Abstract Sounds Books Ltd 2010

Published by Abstract Sounds Books Ltd
Licensed from Archive Media Publishing Ltd
ISBN: 978-0-9566038-3-8

Photography courtesy of Pictorial Press unless otherwise indicated

Contents

THE MAN IN THE MIRROR Michael Jackson **3**

Inside the mind of
Michael Jackson

Fame is something to which many people aspire. From the outside it seems like a never-ending cavalcade of non-stop fun and good times. For many, the achievement of fame represents the highest attainment. Many millions hold the perception that achieving fame will fulfil their deep need to satisfy their egos and enhance their self-esteem. For the vast majority of us, however, the attainment of fame remains an elusive ambition. In some respects that may well be a blessing in disguise, because life in the spotlight can be an extremely lonely place indeed.

The pressure of fame came to Michael Jackson at a particularly early age, and Michael found it hard to cope with the loneliness that came with it. He often spoke about his unhappiness, and famously confided to Oprah Winfrey just how painful the process had been for him. He openly confessed to Oprah live on national TV just how he really felt when fame finally arrived, 'I was lonely, sad, having to face popularity and all that. There were times when I had great times with my brothers, pillow fights and things, but I used to always cry from loneliness.'

It is a sobering experience to review footage of Michael living his life in the full glare of the media spotlight. Replaying the footage of his fraught public appearances can only evoke sympathy, even from his harshest critics. Time and again as we look at the old film rushes we witness the same frenzied excitement, invariably leading to him being mobbed. Almost as soon as the footage of him going about his business begins to run, viewers immediately begin to experience the first glimmers of an understanding of what it meant to live his life in such an intense media spotlight.

With his colossal record sales and worldwide fan base, Michael had achieved fame on an altogether different scale than almost any other celebrity. He appealed equally to members of both sexes. His was an appeal which transcended all racial, national, political, and ethnic barriers. He was almost always the most important person in any room he entered, and all eyes were always upon him, putting him at the centre of the type of media scrums which only form around the extremely famous. Diana, Princess of Wales, was perhaps the only other public figure to inspire such devotion and intense scrutiny. David Beckham is another celebrity who has experienced similar feeding frenzies, but Michael was a much bigger star, and the result was a constant crush of well-wishers and a media entourage following him everywhere he went in the world.

The fans and the accompanying press pack would inevitably assemble outside Michael's hotel and maintain a ceaseless vigil, chanting his name endlessly and dogging his every waking moment. We need to bear in mind that this happened not just in his native North America, but all around the globe; it happened all over Europe, in Japan, in the Philippines, in the UK, and in Asia. He couldn't escape his celebrity even in Africa. On every single occasion that he stepped into the outside world the word would spread like wildfire, and as a result he constantly found himself hounded by a huge press of humanity.

If we take a minute to study the archive footage closely, it is a simple exercise to project ourselves into Michael's position and view the world from his perspective. When we step into his shoes we quickly realise how daunting and frightening such an experience would have been. To be confronted constantly by those lenses, flashing light bulbs, clicking shutters, and cameramen jostling for position, to have those big cameras constantly thrust in our faces would be an extremely disorienting, unnerving, threatening, and dangerous experience. If we add a hard core of fans who are constantly screaming out our name and attempting to touch us to that mix it becomes obvious that this was a shockingly difficult life, indeed.

There was nothing pleasant for Michael about appearing in public. From the hysteria it provoked amongst the media and public alike, even the simplest shopping expedition was invariably a tense and distressing experience. People naturally aspire to be famous, but when one begins to look at the reality of what it was like for Michael Jackson as a superstar, experiencing life on an altogether different level of celebrity, it is immediately apparent that he led an extremely difficult life, indeed.

Not knowing who to trust and not knowing to whom he could speak openly or to whom he could hand his finances inevitably contributed to making him an inward-looking person. It is clear from the events in his

6 Michael Jackson **THE MAN IN THE MIRROR**

life that introspection, with the same thoughts going round and round the things in his head, caused a number of mental-health problems to manifest themselves. The cumulative effect of these factors was that he was never be able to express or show his true identity and inevitably became intensely inward in his persona. The Michael we see in the footage shows clear indications of high levels of stress and anxiety.

One form of coping behaviour in such situations is to develop a public persona and a different private persona, a device which Michael frequently used, slipping in and out of whichever personality he needed in order to please whatever person or particular media form in front of him. He employed this talent often as the events of his truly remarkable life began to unfold.

The early days

In 1964, six-year-old Michael, along with his brother Marlon, joined the ranks of the Jackson Brothers, a group which three of his older brothers – Jacky, Tito, and Jermaine – had originally formed. Michael and Marlon had initially joined as extra percussionists, performing on congas and tambourines, but it soon became apparent that Michael had an exceptional talent, and by 1966 he was a member of the full line-up and had already begun to assume the role of lead vocalist. As a consequence, they changed the group's name from the Jackson Brothers to the Jackson 5.

They became popular performers in their native Chicago, and from the age of eight onwards Michael really had no childhood, missing out on the ordinary formative experiences which most of us take for granted, and was unable to grow up as a normal child whilst being groomed to take his place as the lead singer of a pop group. Life inside the entertainment world is far removed from the ordinary, highly routine life of a normal schoolchild, and from the age of eight he was performing and appearing in what was termed the chitlin-circuit clubs around Chicago.

Not having a regular childhood had a huge effect on Michael as an adult. Losing his childhood was a theme to which he often returned in interviews, and it was to have an enormous effect on him. Being thrust into that relentless media goldfish bowl from the time he was eight was even harder on him, for from then on he enjoyed no privacy at any time in any aspect of his life outside of his home up to his death at the age of 50. That was inevitably a catastrophic factor contributing to the state of his mental health.

Michael
and his family

Michael's father, Joseph (Joe) Jackson, was the driving force behind the Jackson 5. Joe was a steelworker who had raised a large family with his wife Katherine in Gary, Indiana, a hard-working industrial suburb of Chicago. By day he worked hard in a steel mill, but his true love was music, and he was a keen semi-professional musician, performing along with his brother Luther in a local R&B band called the Falcons. Katherine Jackson was a devout churchgoer, and the nine Jackson children were raised as Jehovah's Witnesses.

Joe Jackson seems to have been a hard taskmaster. He had an absolutely clear vision for what he wanted to achieve with his talented family, and it was this overriding drive to succeed that led to some of the difficulties which Michael was to experience in later life. Michael stated in numerous interviews that his father had been abusive towards him and that this abuse took two forms.

First of all were physical beatings, which would obviously have left their mark on what appears to have been a sensitive and delicate personality. More importantly, Joe frequently tormented Michael about his physical appearance, something which also appears to have left lasting mental scars. In retrospect, Joe's disciplinary methods do seem severe by any standard.

Marlon later described how Joe held Michael upside down by one leg and, according to Marlon, pummelled him over and over again on his back and buttocks with his hand. Joe himself gave an interview for the BBC in 2003 in which he confirmed that such incidents as this were frequent. Joe's violent outbursts were largely the result of his efforts to polish first the Jackson Brothers and then the Jackson 5 into a strong professional unit, as it was his habit to force them into what for young children must have seemed to be endless rehearsals. He also appears to have had a short temper, which frightened Michael well into adulthood.

These interludes cast a cloud over Michael's relationship with his father. On being pressed by Oprah Winfrey in his famous 1993 live interview, he revealed something of his true state of mind concerning Joe Jackson by saying, 'Sometimes I do get angry. I don't know him the way I'd like to know him. I just wish I could understand my father.'

Michael's distrust of his father became all too apparent many years later, when his will made no mention of Joe Jackson when it became public after his death.

> *I had pimples so badly it used to make me so shy. I used not to look at myself. I'd hide my face in the dark, I wouldn't want to look in the mirror and my father teased me and I just hated it and I cried everyday.*
>
> OPRAH WINFREY INTERVIEW 1993

Plastic **surgery**

It's often been said that that Michael underwent so much plastic surgery as a result of his flawed personality. He clearly had a number of mental-health issues to manage. He always said that his father had abused him with name-calling and by undermining him, as well as with the physical beatings, and one of the things that he said his father had always teased him about was his looks, telling him often that he was ugly.

It's possible that this may be reading too much into that, but it clearly left a mark on him, and if he actually did feel that he was ugly, once he'd made his fortune he had no obstacle to resorting to repeated plastic surgery. The effects of his father's taunts and plastic surgery may also explain his strange preference for being seen in public wearing a mask.

In an interview on 1 July 2009, chartered psychologist Sarah Jackson said, 'There has inevitably been great speculation on what's behind his fondness for plastic surgery. You could possibly take from it the fact that he was constantly seeking to change his persona, change his perception of himself, and of how others viewed him as well. It could also be about trying to re-invent himself to keep up with his changing career. He almost became a new person with each new record.

'From the outside it appears as if he was constantly seeking to resolve something that wasn't right in his life, an unmet need. Something wasn't right, so he would go and have something fixed; he would come back and try and re-invent himself again.

'It could have been something about control. He lacked the ability to trust so many others in his life, so that could be an aspect as well. It was something he could do and keep to himself and have full control over that aspect of his life.

'Again, there are a couple of arguments for this. If you look back, he suggests a lot that while he was a child his father called him ugly, and he was quite unsure about the way he was and the verbal abuse he got, and he really didn't like the way he looked. The mask could just have been a way for him to cover up preceding the plastic surgery. It could also have been a cry for attention. He wasn't a stupid man. He knew how to work the media and it would ultimately get him attention, be it good or bad.'

Drawing upon the things he later had to say concerning his father's harsh words, a number of commentators have speculated that he may have suffered from a condition called body dysmorphic disorder. Others have speculated that he may have actually been engaging in a process akin to self-harming.

This is a theory which, in her own study of Michael, Sarah Jackson does not discount, explaining, 'Self-harm is a form of addiction, and it's suggested that it's the anticipation of the process rather than the event which is the most important aspect. The other thing with self-harm which keeps people addicted is of course the natural pain killers that kick in, the endorphins, as a result of the self-harming. It could be parallel to plastic surgery, that constant search to undergo a process which produces endorphins. What keeps someone addicted to self-harm are these natural pain killers, the endorphins, which kick in as an end result of the harming, and one can obtain a similar kind of sensation from plastic surgery.

'There's also the ability that they can do that to themselves; it's a control thing. Self-harmers know they can do it; they are in control and invariably no one else can stop them. Plastic surgery would have given him a sense of control over at least one aspect of his life. Addiction itself is a clinical condition that can be applied across a broad spectrum from any behaviour or activity, basically, that is compulsive, that's adverse to their lifestyle or personality. Addiction can be seen in disorders with regard to obvious things, such as alcohol, drugs, or food, but it can also be applied to excessive exercise and, indeed, self-harming, and plastic surgery could be included in that category.'

> ## "My father was a management genius. But what I really wanted was a dad."
>
> SPEECH AT OXFORD UNION, ON SUBJECT OF CHILD WELFARE.

14 Michael Jackson **THE MAN IN THE MIRROR**

Child **fame**

t is widely accepted that the difficult environment of life as a child performer robbed Michael of his childhood. This was certainly the view that he took, and evidence certainly supports that conclusion. By 1966, when Michael was only eight years old, the Jackson 5 were working hard on the Midwest chitlin circuit of black clubs and venues.

On the same circuit at the time was a little-known guitarist named Jimi Hendrix, but despite the calibre of many of the performers, the clubs were not wholly concerned with music and were certainly unsuitable places for youngsters. They would often find themselves as the opening act for comedians and even strip shows.

The Jackson 5 received their first commercial break in 1967, when they were signed to the local Steeltown label. The group recorded several songs, including the rather ironically titled 'Big Boy', without achieving any notable success. However, fame was just around the corner, and the Steeltown learning curve proved to be a valuable experience. In 1968 they switched labels from Steeltown to Motown, and the path to fame and stardom lay open to them.

Life on the road was a far from ideal start for Michael at an age when the human brain is at a crucial formative stage, and leading such an organised, regimented life would have been likely to stifle his independent development.

Sarah Jackson expanded on the potential problems of growing up in an environment in which someone controlled his every move for someone like Michael by

> *In the end, the most important thing is to be true to yourself and those you love and work hard. Work like there's no tomorrow. Train. Strive. Really train and cultivate your talent to the highest degree. Be the best at what you do.*

explaining, 'The brain is a very complex organ, and it is primarily there to problem-solve, to think things through, to find ways to get control and get needs met. If someone is constantly doing that for you, parts of the brain aren't being used. Neglect leads to neural connections being lost, and we lose the ability to perform those particular functions altogether. This state of dependency can cause all sorts of mental problems. It can lead to depression, anxiety problems, problems with managing stress; coping skills for life get diminished.'

As we know from his own account, Michael suffered from loneliness and cried a great deal. Nonetheless, his off-stage problems did not manifest themselves in his on-stage world. He quickly emerged as the group's main focus, being the lead singer and also exhibiting an amazing talent as a dancer.

Motown was a great home for the group, and the Jackson 5 enjoyed success from the start. Their first four singles recorded for Motown – 'I Want You Back,' 'ABC,' 'The Love You Save,' and 'I'll Be There' – all reached the number-one spot on the Billboard Hot 100. By the time the last single hit the charts, Michael was 11 years old and heading towards adolescence. He no longer presented the cute figure of a child star. For some reason, Motown's marketing brains decided that it would be a good idea to claim that he was actually only nine.

The problem of not being able be open with the

world was beginning to make a mark on Michael. 'It was very, very difficult,' he once said, 'because I think every child star suffers through this period because you're not the cute and charming child that you were. You start to grow, and they want to keep you little forever.'

It soon became obvious that Michael's talent was such that it could not be contained within the ranks of the group, and in 1972 he began his solo career, which was to take him to the very peak of the music industry. He released four solo albums with Motown, the most notable of which was the enormous, top-selling Ben, which contained the hit single of the same name. It was another indication of the enormous talent which lay awaiting its moment to really shine, but it was a talent that had been nurtured at the expense of such vital things as a normal childhood.

The psychological effects of missing out on that childhood were to become apparent in Michael's behaviour later in life, as he sought to discover the childlike state through his infatuation with theme parks. He was an obsessive enthusiast of funfairs, and this of course reached a peak with his purchase of the Neverland Ranch and its infamous funfair.

Michael's yearning for a return to a lost childhood could also be seen in the childlike friendships that he formed with such other child stars as Macauly Caulkin, who similarly felt that he had lost his childhood. In some respects this may well explain his attachment to Elizabeth Taylor, who'd been a child star and who would

have been sympathetic to his lost childhood. Of course, the two shared an even deeper understanding through their mutual difficulties with prescription drugs.

Most of the downside to the Jackson 5's success would not become apparent for many years, and from 1972 through 1975 they continued to enjoy top-40 hits on the Motown label, although it was noticeable that their overall success rate was beginning to decline. As a consequence of this they moved to CBS Records in 1975. The switch from Motown to CBS was not without its problems, and legal action resulted in the group changing its name from the Jackson 5 to the Jacksons. Legal issues such as this would have highlighted some of his inevitable issues of trust, which stayed with him all his life.

According to Sarah Jackson, 'For Michael in particular that was something that he learned at quite a young age. He probably found that he had to keep things very much to himself. Not knowing who he could turn to, who he could trust, would have affected his mental condition. Pretty much anyone he came into contact with were pursuing him, so he would have been very much always on guard – what he could say, what he could do – which would have changed his whole identity. He probably would have ended up not even knowing his identity himself. That would always be the risk.'

The name switch did little to harm the group, and the Jacksons went on to release six albums between 1976

18 Michael Jackson **THE MAN IN THE MIRROR**

Because I think every child star suffers through this period because you're not the cute and charming child that you were. You start to grow, and they want to keep you little forever.

OPRAH WINFREY INTERVIEW 1993

and 1984. By that time Michael had grown in prominence as a result of his successful solo career and being the Jacksons' lead songwriter, writing a string of such hits as, 'Shake Your Body (Down to the Ground),' 'This Place Hotel,' and 'Can You Feel It?'

In 1979 Michael broke his nose when he fell awkwardly during a complex dance routine that he was

> *There is a lot of sadness in my past life. My father beat me. He was strict; very hard and stern.*

preparing in order to be featured in the live show to promote his new album, Off the Wall. Off the Wall became a real breakthrough, and is still widely regarded as a masterpiece. However, the surgery on his broken nose was less than satisfactory, and he decided that a second rhinoplasty was necessary. This led to many subsequent operations, which of course provoked

never-ending controversy.

Michael and Quincy Jones jointly produced Off the Wall, which featured such special guests as Stevie Wonder and Paul McCartney. Although it only reached number three on the Billboard 200, it has become a strong seller over the years, and by now has sold an estimated more than 20 million copies.

The 1980s were to prove a particularly fruitful decade for Michael, who was reputed to have secured for himself the highest royalty rate in the music industry. The success of his next album, Thriller, justified this, as it became the best-selling, most-played single recording of his career. It spawned seven top-10 singles, including the anthems 'Billie Jean' and 'Beat It,' and has now sold an estimated more than 110 million copies, which easily makes it the best-selling album of all time. Thriller marked the beginning of an extraordinarily lucrative era for him, but unfortunately it also provoked a period of extravagant expenditure, something that was to be one of the hallmarks of his behaviour from then on.

On 25 March 1983 Michael performed his famous moonwalk for the first time in front of 47 million TV viewers. At the time it drew comparisons with the Ed Sullivan appearances by Elvis Presley and the Beatles.

Then, on 27 January 1984, some misplaced pyrotechnics accidentally set fire to Michael's hair while he was filming a Pepsi Cola commercial at the Shrine Auditorium in Los Angeles, resulting in second-degree burns to his scalp. Pepsi settled by paying him $1.5

million compensation, which he unselfishly donated to the Brottman Medical Centre in Culver City, California, which had provided him with treatment following the accident.

Michael seems to have become increasingly concerned about his appearance and underwent his third rhinoplasty, and appeared to grow increasingly self-conscious about it.

In 1984 he co-wrote the charity single 'We are the World' with Lionel Ritchie. It ultimately generated in excess of $20 million dollars for famine relief. During this period he became increasingly friendly with Paul McCartney, working on two hit singles, 'The Girl is Mine' and 'Say, Say, Say.' However, the friendship took a turn for the worse when Michael bought the ATV songs music catalogue, which included all of the Lennon-McCartney classics written between 1963-73. McCartney famously remarked, 'I think its dodgy to do things like that and then buy the rug they're standing on.'

Michael's fame continued to grow throughout the second half of the 1980s, but unfortunately so did his obsession with plastic surgery. He had a fourth rhinoplasty, and in an apparent effort to accentuate the masculine aspect of his visage he had a cleft chin added to his new face. He acquired a huge entourage of hangers-on and advisors, and also a pet chimpanzee named Bubbles. Such eccentricities inspired the popular press to start calling him 'Wacko Jacko.'

Leading a life as if he were a king was less than ideal.

Sarah Jackson highlighted some of the dangers of this by explaining, 'Being constantly pampered and feted makes it very difficult to be mentally healthy in a lot of respects. We all have certain needs that need to be met, and attention, for example, is a prime consideration. Our attention needs can obviously be met in good ways, but it can also be met in some bad ways. Attention is something that we need to give and receive in order to be mentally well. Attention needs sometimes get met negatively as well as positively, and if you become acclimatised to that environment where you receive too much attention it can be a bad thing. To find that one is constantly the centre of attraction can also take away your perceived control if you are always expected to behave in a certain way. It takes that control from you and it almost becomes that you are acting out your life rather than living it.'

Life for Michael in the spotlight was clearly extraordinarily difficult. He was constantly looking at lenses being thrust into his face, the clicking of shutters and flashbulbs going off invaded his world incessantly, and of course he experienced the shrieking and noise of his fans repeatedly calling his name every time he left his home. All this meant that even the most basic exercise of walking down a street in ordinary civilised society was an entirely different experience for him than for ordinary people. Such pressure would soon begin to tell on even the strongest personality, and it must have had a particularly severe effect on his altogether frail psyche .

The footage of an ad hoc 2002 train trip he made with Uri Geller and David Blaine from London to Exeter is among the most revealing views of what it really meant to be Michael Jackson. When people noticed that he was actually in Paddington Station and about to board a train the news spread like wildfire. On the ITN tape we can see that the crush of excited bodies actually knocked him to the ground. He was clearly under physical threat and his life appeared to be in danger.

We can also witness a similar phenomenon on at a trip he made to Moscow when he attempted to do something any tourist there would do and visit Red Square and the Kremlin, something so completely ordinary and mundane that any of us would take it for granted. He clearly just wanted to enjoy a short sightseeing trip, but the footage reveals the truth of the experience through his eyes, showing that as he attempted to leave the car to have a look at Red Square an excited mob immediately surrounded him and the usual frenzy began, forcing him to about-face and make for the car, once again thwarted in the most innocent of ambitions.

In the late 1980s the whole structure of Michael's face appeared to change, and observers speculated that he had undergone multiple nasal surgeries, a forehead lift, lip-thinning, and cheekbone enhancement. A period of severe weight loss accompanied these alterations, leading inevitably to speculation that he was anorexic or that he suffered from body dysmorphic disorder. During the course of the 1990s his skin grew noticeably paler, and eventually he was diagnosed as suffering from vitiligo and lupus, the latter of which was in remission. These combined illnesses made him painfully sensitive to sunlight, and as a result he took to wearing a hat and carrying an umbrella.

Thriller had proved to be a massive and enduring hit, and it took five years before Michael was in a position to unveil its successor, but when the highly anticipated moment arrived it was not a disappointment. Although it sold fewer copies than Thriller, many regard the 1987 album Bad as an all-time classic, especially as it was home to a further seven hit singles, including the eponymous title track and 'Man in the Mirror.' It hit the number-one spot on the Billboard chart and has sold an estimated 50 million copies.

The gold-plated, military-style jacket that Michael wore on stage marked his tour of the album from 12 September 1987 through to 14 January 1989. The entire tour consisted of 123 concerts to a total audience of 4.4 million people, and during the tour's UK leg 504,000 people attended seven shows at Wembley Stadium. During the course of the tour, he regularly invited underprivileged children to attend the concerts for free and visited hospitals and orphanages, making large charitable donations.

Michael and Diana

n 1988 Michael met Diana, Princess of Wales, for the first time, and she was to be a major influence on his life from that point onwards. It's fair to say that Michael's persona had a markedly feminine facet to it, which is obviously one of the reasons why he found it easy to forge friendships with women. However, we need to look much closer at his relationship with Diana in order to understand why the bond between them was so strong. They both lived their lives in the eye of an intense media vortex that deprived them of the ordinary things we all take for granted.

The mutual attraction was understandable, as only someone like Diana could possibly begin to understand the pressures of being forced by fame to live one's whole life in the goldfish bowl of publicity, having been forced to endure an existence at the centre of the same sort of media frenzy as that which surrounded Michael.

When Michael eventually met Diana for the first time in 1988, it was clearly an enormously momentous moment for him, because at last he'd found a kindred spirit. It was almost inconceivable, but she was about as famous as he was, so for the first time he didn't have to be the most famous person in the room. It is fascinating to look at the footage of that historic first meeting in 1988. In it we can actually see him for once having to take his place in the receiving line. He was clearly not the most important figure in that room. It must have been a marvellously pleasant experience for him not to have all of the glare of publicity on him alone for once.

He would have been extraordinarily sympathetic to Diana's plight with media pressure, and the bond between them would have been instant, as both could understand the realities of their situations in a way that he couldn't really communicate with anyone else.

Michael
and Elizabeth

It should be no surprise that the other person who played such a big part in Michael's life was, of course, Elizabeth Taylor. Again, she was somebody who had been a child star and who had lived her life entirely in the glare of publicity, again presenting a natural bond with him. Elizabeth did much to help him through his life.

Understanding the pressures confronting him, when he became addicted to prescription drugs it was Elizabeth who stood up and helped take some of the pressure off his slender shoulders by accepting the burden of going in front of the media and publicly telling the world about the kind of stress that he was experiencing. Facing the media on his behalf was indeed an enormous favour, but she understood, as someone who'd been under similar pressures herself, how important it was that she help him, and that it was necessary to explain to the world exactly what he was going through.

In 1988 Michael released his first autobiography, entitled Moonwalk, which told of his early experiences in the Jackson 5 and the abuse he had suffered at the hands of his father. In the same year he purchased land near Santa Ynez, California, upon which he built the Neverland Ranch.

In 1991 Michael renewed his contract with Sony, which had purchased CBS, and received a record-breaking $65 million advance. The advance was justified by the release of the album Dangerous in 1991, which has since gone on to sell in the region of 35 million copies worldwide. Its first single, 'Black or White', reached number one on the US Billboard chart. Its other singles included 'Remember the Time' and 'Heal the World.' As a result of that single he founded the Heal the World Foundation, a charity which brought children to Neverland, where they could enjoy its theme-park rides. It has also spent millions of dollars around the world to help children threatened by war and disease.

> *Elizabeth Taylor is gorgeous, beautiful, and she still is today, I'm crazy about her.*
>
> OPRAH WINFREY INTERVIEW 1993

Elizabeth Taylor at the American Film Festival of Deauville (Normandy, France) in September 1985

Michael began the Dangerous world tour to support the album on 27 June 1992. By the time it eventually came to a conclusion on 11 November 1993, he had performed to over 3.5 million fans in an extended run of 67 concerts. The concerts were not solely for the benefit of record sales, though, as he donated all the tour's profits directly to the Heal the World Foundation. He sold the tour's broadcast rights to HBO for $20 million, which was then a record-breaking deal for a single music event.

In addition to his work with the Heal the World Foundation, he was also influential early in the campaign to draw attention to the dangers posed by HIV/AIDS. It should be borne in mind that this good work was done at a time when the disease was relatively unknown and was still something of a political issue.

Michael **and charity**

It seems that all celebrities living their lives in the public eye sooner or later want to be seen to be doing work on behalf of charity. Show business performers are natural show-offs. They need approbation and acclaim. Inevitably the cynic in us suggests that some celebrities appear at charity events simply in order to raise their profiles.

However, one thing of which we can be certain is that Michael had no need for to raise his profile; he was already the most famous man on the planet. He was absolutely sincere about his charity work. For example, if we listen to the speech that he made at Exeter City Football Club in 2002, we can immediately understand how passionate he was about the need to do charitable work for children. He genuinely believed that he had a responsibility and a duty to help others who found themselves in difficulty. His work on behalf of children was truly charitable work that raised huge sums.

We should also remember that he continued to do this work at a time when he was not always in the best shape himself. When he went to Russia the Russian state honoured him for the work he did for charity. When he went to South Africa, Nelson Mandela himself took the time to address the press about his admiration for Michael Jackson. A person would have to be astronomically cynical indeed not to believe that he was involved in charity work for the best possible motives. He genuinely wanted to help and felt that he had a duty to do so.

Michael's main public energies focused on his work

> *Everything that I love is behind those gates. We have elephants and giraffes and crocodiles, and every kind of tigers and lions. And we have bus loads of kids, who don't get to see those things. They come up sick children and enjoy it.*

DESCRIBING NEVERLAND RANCH IN CALIFORNIA, CBS INTERVIEW 2003

for charity, and it was unusual for him to step outside of that and become embroiled in a political concern, but he did become involved in politics when he started to speak out on behalf of black artists in the music industry. At the time of his dispute with Sony he joined a crusade led by the Reverend Al Sharpton, becoming highly critical of attitudes towards black artists in the music industry.

By speaking out strongly on behalf of black artists he ignited a most public campaign targeting Sony Records. Being already in a dispute with Sony fired his enthusiasm. He outspokenly criticised Tommy Mottola, the head of Sony, on deeply personal grounds, publicly accusing him of being a racist. It was obvious that Mottola was certainly not a racist, but Michael drew that conclusion from what he perceived to be a conflict of interest. He felt so strongly about that issue that he felt compelled to come out and make that statement.

Now, there was plenty of bad blood between Michael and Sony, and, helped by Al Sharpton, he constantly milked his position for all it was worth. It resulted in many members of the public embarking on a curious boycott of Sony, which showed some of the power that he actually wielded. It also showed that he could be a political campaigner if he chose to do so.

Michael's celebrated trip to Africa also demonstrated his desire to do good work. The hysteria surrounding his visit to the Ivory Coast,

Gabon, and Egypt was enormous, and massive crowds flocked to welcome him, often bearing aloft signs reading 'Welcome Home Michael.' One bizarre incident involved the world press being summoned to witness him being crowned 'King SA I' in the Ivory Coast, with a tribal chief presiding over the ceremony. Sitting on a golden throne, Michael signed some official documents and thanked his hosts in both French and English.

Back in the US, Michael marked his stellar status with a halftime performance at Superbowl XXVII. The truncated set included just four songs, 'Jam,' 'Billie Jean,' 'Black or White,' and 'Heal the World.' It is interesting to note that his popularity was so overwhelming that this was the first superbowl telecast during which the halftime audience figures actually increased, his performance being seen by 135 million people in America and an estimated 350 million worldwide. One effect of the appearance was an enormous upsurge in album sales, but he still kept the focus on his charity work with the inclusion of 'Heal the World.'

In 1993 Michael's world began to fall apart. It began well enough with the celebrated 90-minute interview with Oprah Winfrey in February. This live appearance marked his first television interview since 1979, and he gave a remarkably candid insight into his life, touching upon his feeling that he'd missed his childhood and had suffered what he considered to be mental and physical abuse at the hands of his father. He took the opportunity to deny widely held suspicions that he had bleached his skin by stating for the first time that he suffered from a condition known as vitiligo that causes pigmentation difficulties and made his skin appear blotchy.

The bombshell, which followed soon on the heels of the Oprah interview, was the accusation by a 13-year-old boy named Jordan Chandler that Jackson had sexually abused him.

> *I've helped many many, many children, thousands of children, cancer kids, leukemia kids.*
>
> CBS 60 MINUTES INTERVIEW 2003

The Jordan Chandler affair

A year after he first met Michael, and under the influence of a sedative drug called sodium amytal, Jordan Chandler stated that Michael had touched his penis. He said this under questioning by his father, Evan Chandler, who had administered the drug. Armed with this information, Mr Chandler began a series of negotiations to resolve the issue by a financial settlement.

These negotiations, however, could not be concluded, as an official police investigation began immediately, and Michael soon found himself facing both civil and criminal proceedings. Under questioning by a psychiatrist, and also by police, Jordan stated that he and Michael had engaged in acts of kissing, masturbation, and oral sex. Jordan made a point of attempting to substantiate the claims by giving a detailed description of Michael's private parts. In a humiliating and demeaning episode Michael underwent an examination by doctors who concluded that there were strong similarities between his genitalia and the description Jordan had given, but the study was inconclusive.

As part of the search for evidence of criminal activity the police turned over Neverland Ranch thoroughly looking for clues to substantiate Jordan's allegations. Michael's sister LaToya didn't help his case by publicly denouncing him as a paedophile. This public betrayal by LaToya was a major blow to him. That his own sister had

effectively knifed him in the back must have been a crushing blow to his fragile mental state. As anyone would do at such times, Michael obviously relied on his family to support him and nurture him through such a difficult period, so when someone as close as his own sister came out and publicly accused him of being a child molester, something that he always vehemently denied, it must have been a terrific blow to his self-esteem.

His subsequent acquittal in a court of law of similar allegations in 2005, and LaToya's withdrawal of the slur, must have lifted a huge weight from his shoulders. If a court finds a person not guilty, then that person is not guilty, but the damage often lingers.

It is not surprising that Jackson found solace in the prescription drugs valium, xanax, and ativan, something, as noted earlier, Elizabeth Taylor publicly admitted for him in 1993, explaining that she too had been the victim of a similar addiction.

The stress brought on by the case and his mounting addiction caused Michael to cancel the remainder of the Dangerous world tour, and he voluntarily entered a drug-rehabilitation programme. Another side effect of his stressful condition was the onset of an eating disorder that caused him to lose a considerable amount of weight. His legal team have always maintained that it was only as a result of his frail mental and physical condition that he settled the Chandler civil case out of court, even though doing this led to the inevitable media speculation that he had been guilty all along. In the wake of the $22 million settlement Jordan refused to continue with the criminal proceedings and the charges against Michael were dropped, the state closing its criminal investigation due to lack of evidence.

> *Why can't you share your bed? The most loving thing to do is to share your bed with someone. It's very charming. It's very sweet. It's what the whole world should do.*

Lisa Marie **Presley**

Setting aside the stress and strain of an extremely difficult year, in May 1994 Jackson married Lisa Marie Presley, Elvis Presley's daughter. The couple had known each other since 1975, but had been reconnected only in early 1993. Lisa Marie provided him with huge support during the Jordan Chandler affair and his fight against his addiction to prescription drugs. She had, of course, witnessed the effects of a similar addiction on her own father, and she would have been particularly alive to the consequences.

Lisa Marie and Michael married secretly in the Dominican Republic and, bizarrely, after their marriage continued to deny they were a couple. Some have speculated that their marriage was merely a cover-up operation, with Lisa Marie stating publicly that it was 'sexually active.' Sadly the union was not destined to last. They separated in 1995 and divorced in 1996.

In 1995 Michael sold half of his interest in the Northern Songs catalogue to Sony/ATV Music Publishing, which provided him with a much-needed $95 million advance that went some way toward easing some of the money problems which had dogged his footsteps as a result of his tendency to overspend. At about that time he also released a double album called HIStory: Past, Present and Future, Book One, which featured a greatest-hits selection on disc one and 15 new songs on disc two.

Despite all that had happened to him the album debuted at number one in the charts and has since gone on to sell 50 million copies. The first single from the album, 'Scream,' was a duet Michael performed with his youngest sister, Janet. The second single, 'You Are Not Alone,' debuted at number one in the Billboard top

100, and the third single, 'Earth Song', proved to be his most successful single in many overseas territories and has sold an estimated million copies in the UK alone.

In 1996 Michael entered into more controversy when the Anti-Defamation League accused him of anti-Semitism because the original lyrics of the song 'They Don't Care About Us' had originally included the lines, 'Jew me, sue me' and 'Kick me, kike me.' Under pressure from the league, he relented and stated that he would re-record the lyrics before the album went into production. The dispute over the lyrics caused problems for him with his many Jewish friends, such as Steven Spielberg.

> "*I slept in a bed with all of them when Macauley Culkin was little: Kieran Culkin would sleep on this side, Macauley Culkin was on this side, his sisters in there...we all would just jam in the bed, you know.*"
>
> MARTIN BASHIR INTERVIEW, "LIVING WITH MICHAEL JACKSON", ITV

The death of **Diana**

In August 1997 Michael suffered a huge blow when he learned of Princess Diana's death, which appeared to have had a catastrophic effect on him. Despite the traumatic effects of Princess Diana's death, he remained strong enough to begin the HIStory world tour. It began on 7 September 1997 and finished over a year later on 15 October 1998. During that time he performed 82 concerts in 58 cities for audiences totalling more than 4.5 million fans, making it the most successful of all his tours in terms of audience figures.

It was during the Australian leg of the HIStory tour that another remarkable event occurred. Michael met up with and married an Australian dermatology nurse called Deborah Jeanne Rowe, who bore him his first two children. These were a son named Michael Joseph Jackson Junior, known to Michael as Prince, and a daughter named Paris Michael Katherine Jackson.

He'd first met Deborah in the mid-1980s at a time when he'd first been diagnosed with vitiligo. As a specialist skin nurse, Deborah had spent many years treating his illness, and the romance had grown from there. Many think that they originally had no plans to marry and that they only did so with the news of Deborah's first pregnancy, due to his mother Katherine's strong religious convictions.

They finally divorced in 1999, with Deborah accepting a settlement giving full custody rights of the children to Michael, but they nonetheless remained on strongly friendly terms afterwards.

1997 marked the release of Blood on the Dance Floor: HIStory in the Mix, which was a strange affair containing remixes of the singles from HIStory accompanied by five new songs. This was, not

The funeral of Diana, Princess of Wales. Diana's tragic death had a massive impact on Michael

surprisingly, to prove the weakest-selling album of Michael's recording career with Sony, but world sales nonetheless now stand at about 10 million copies. Although it reached number one in the UK, it only attained number 24 on the Billboard chart.

Despite Michael's enormous commercial success, money worries continued to dog him throughout the 1990s. A popular joke was that he was a millionaire with a billionaire's tastes and habits, and to an extent this may have been accurate. His income in 1977 was an estimated $20 million, but his expenditures were probably almost double that.

Despite his personal problems Michael continued to do as much charitable work as he could, and in conjunction with Luciano Pavorotti he performed at a benefit for the War Child Foundation that raised a million dollars for Kosovo refugees. Later in 1999 he organised the first of the Michael Jackson and Friends benefit concerts, which took place in Germany and Korea. Such other artists as Slash, the Scorpions, Boyz II Men, Luther Vandross, Mariah Carey, and of course Luciano Pavorotti were involved. The proceeds from the concerts were donated to the Nelson Mandela Children's Fund, the Red Cross, and UNESCO. Despite all his good works, he continued to be plagued by newspaper allegations, and in an effort to set the record straight he gave an interview to the Daily Mirror in which he attempted to turn the tide of hatred against him.

> *Let us dream of tomorrow where we can truly love from the soul, and know love as the ultimate truth at the heart of all creation.*

Problems with **Sony**

> *I'm a black American, I am proud of my race. I am proud of who I am. I have a lot of pride and dignity.*

The new millennium began with fresh turmoil for Michael. He became embroiled in a contract dispute with Sony Music Entertainment, and, as mentioned earlier, accused Tommy Mattola, Sony's CEO, of being a racist as a result of his attitude towards black artists. One consequence of this was that he was able to use these conflicts as leverage to exit his contract early.

Sony appeared to respond by reducing the level of promotion for the Invincible album, although Sony strongly disputed these claims. Despite all of this backroom fighting Sony released Invincible in 2001.

Michael had been working on the album since 1999 and was keenly enthusiastic about it, something he discussed at length in his interview with the Daily

Mirror that year. In order to promote the album, he appeared at a special celebration at Madison Square Garden in New York to mark his thirtieth anniversary as a solo artist. Ironically, he made his first appearance alongside his brothers since 1984 at this celebration.

Invincible was a major commercial success. It debuted at number one in 13 countries and has gone on to sell 15 million copies worldwide as of this writing, but by Michael's standards its sales were disappointing. This may well have been due to Sony indeed putting on a half-hearted promotional campaign, but it was more probably due to this time Michael making no world tour to support the album. It's also interesting to note that the third single taken from the album, Butterflies, was one of the first singles he'd released without the benefit of a supporting music video.

In 2002 Michael's third child, rather confusingly named Prince Michael Jackson II, but more commonly known as Blanket, was born to a mother whose identity has never been revealed. Michael has always maintained that the child was born as a result of artificial insemination of a surrogate mother with his donated sperm. In November 2002 he took the unwise step of dangling the baby over the balcony of a Berlin hotel room, and was later forced to apologise for the incident, which he described as 'a terrible mistake.'

> *I love my children. I was holding my son tight. Why would I throw a baby off the balcony? That's the dumbest, stupidest story I ever heard.*

More child abuse **allegations**

Michael gave a glaringly open account of his private life to interviewer Martin Bashir in the infamous 2003 Grenada Television documentary entitled Living with Michael Jackson. It was first time that he discussed his relationship with a young boy named Gavin Arvizo. Shortly after the documentary aired he found himself charged with seven counts of child sexual abuse involving Gavin.

This marked the beginning of another painfully difficult period for Michael, who always denied the allegations and maintained that the sleeping arrangements were not sexual.

Elizabeth Taylor once again came to his aid, defending him powerfully on the Larry King Live TV show, where she told about actually being together with Michael and some children in bed watching television, and as far as she was concerned there was nothing abnormal in this behaviour, explaining, 'There was no touchy-feely going on. We laughed like children, and we watched a lot of Walt Disney. There was nothing odd about it.'

One objective view of Michael's behaviour at the time came from Dr Stan Katz, a state-appointed clinical and forensic psychologist, who spent a considerable length of time interviewing both Michael and Gavin and came to the conclusion that Michael had regressed mentally to a 10-year-old mindset and that he certainly did not fit the traditional profile of a paedophile.

Sarah Jackson shares that view, explaining that, 'The

> *It's a complete lie, why do people buy these papers? It's not the truth I'm here to say. You know, don't judge a person, do not pass judgement, unless you have talked to them one on one. I don't care what the story is, do not judge them because it is a lie.*

evidence would certainly suggest that that would have been the case. When he was interviewed on several occasions he was very open in his relationship with children, and my opinion would be that, yes, his wanting to be with children was innocent. It was a chance for him to get back the childhood he had lost and to live that life. He felt a certain affinity to children; he did the same thing with animals. He could be sure that he was not being judged and he could trust those relationships. They were very open, they were very black-and-white, and he could just be himself; he didn't have to take on an identity of any form.'

The People v Jackson trial finally began in 2005 in Santa Maria, California. During the run-up to the trial Michael had progressed from prescription drugs to a reliance upon morphine. His appearance was increasingly frail, but he strongly maintained his innocence. The jury acquitting him on all charges provided him with vindication. After the trial he relocated to the Persian Gulf island of Bahrain, where he stayed as the guest of Sheik Abdullah.

Unfortunately Michael will be forever associated with the whole murky business of children and child abuse, even though after a rigorous and lengthy trial an all-white jury found him not guilty. Still, the cumulative effects of the Jordan Chandler and Gavin Arvizo scandals have been such that those allegations will always put a cloud over his memory. That's a great shame, as he had a genuine desire to help children and to make their lives better, raising countless millions for children's charities.

In footage from the news archives of the world's press we can see Michael all over the world visiting children's hospitals, raising money for children's charities, and doing his absolute best to do good works everywhere he went. This desire to help children may well have been a symptom of Dr Katz's diagnosis that he was a child who had never really grown up. If we consider carefully the implications of him having a funfair built on the grounds of his own house we can't help but understand just how childlike he really was. He visited Disneyland in California many times, and also visited Disneylands in Japan and Europe. It was the kind of activity that most men approaching 50 have long put behind them, but for him the world of attractions and theme parks held a magic that he obviously lacked in his own life and was trying hard to capture by regressing to a childlike state.

Sarah Jackson pointed to how his behaviour mirrored this, explaining that, 'There's a lot of support for that argument if you think that Michael Jackson really was forced to be an adult, really, from the age of about five. Child development is very important for the adult psyche. It sets about how you respond and behave in life, and sometimes an adult can reflect back and seek to re-experience those childhood states. Then, of course, there's Neverland and the attraction to children and the

way they behave. He obviously wanted to be a part of that in his behaviour, and in his actual words we hear him saying, "I want to get that time back, but I want my second childhood to be what I want it to be." If you look at Michael Jackson's life, there are a lot of parallels to

> *"Please keep an open mind and let me have my day in court.*

child behaviour – the excessive spending, the innocence in the way he conducts himself. It's very much a child in the sweetshop syndrome, only with a platinum American Express. If he wanted it, he could have it. That childhood part of his brain would kick in and he would spend.'

No matter what, the most powerful thing in the world is the human mind and prayer, and belief in yourself and confidence and perseverance. No matter how many times you do it, you do it again until it's right. And always believe in yourself.

The Nation of **Islam**

As Michael prepared for his trial in 2004, he appointed Leonard Mohammed, the chief of staff of the Nation of Islam, as his new business manager. From that point onwards his affairs became closely enmeshed with the Nation of Islam, which provided his bodyguards and rented him his new home from their inventory of properties. Still, reports that he was experiencing severe financial problems continue to grow, and in 2006 the main house on the Neverland Ranch had to be closed as a cost-cutting measure.

Then the news emerged that Michael was unable to make the repayments on a $270 million loan which he had secured against his music publishing holdings. This forced him into a re-financing deal backed by Sony that gave Sony the option to buy 50% of his stock in their jointly owned publishing company, leaving him with a personal stake of just 25%. However, by 2006 his musical career was back on track

He could be considered the most successful entertainer of all time, having sold over 100 million albums. His massive success raised issues over who he could trust in his personal life and for legal advice, financial advice, and career advice. He was aware that he was the source of the creativity upon which everyone else around him relied. Everyone with whom he came into contact wanted something from him, and he was acutely aware of this.

Michael's business dealings from 2004 also appeared to return to form, and some of his acquisitions appear to have been shrewd. For example, he and Sony acquired Famous Music LLC from Viacom, providing him with a share in the rights to songs by Eminem, Shakira, Bek, and a host of others.

To celebrate Michael's 50th birthday, Sony BMG released a compilation album called King of Pop. Although it was not released in the US, King of Pop made it into the top 10 in all the countries where it was actually issued. On 21 November 2008 another major shift occurred in his private life. Newspaper reports began to circulate that he had converted to Islam. He had become friendly with the British performer Yusef Islam, who had formerly used the stage name Cat Stevens before converting to Islam in 1977. Interestingly, Michael was not prepared to comment publicly about these reports, although he was reportedly heavily influenced by his brother Jermaine's conversion to Islam in 1989 and was living in Bahrain, a Muslim country.

Michael's highly publicised money problems rumbled on into 2008, and Fortress Investments considered a foreclosure sale on Neverland Ranch as a result of his failure to service a loan he had secured with the property. They reached a solution in which the title to Neverland Ranch was transferred to a company known as Sycamore Valley Ranch Company LLC, with Michael receiving a smaller portion of the ranch's ownership.

In 2009 Michael announced that he would perform a string of 50 concerts at London O2 arena, which were due to start on Monday 13 July and run through to 6 March 2010. Randy Phillips, the president and CEO of AEG Live, stated that Michael would have earned something in the region of £500 million from the string of dates, which were merely the beginning of a four-year plan that included a world tour and recording and releasing new music.

> *If you enter this world knowing you are loved and you leave this world knowing the same, then everything that happens in between can be dealt with.*

The death of
Michael Jackson

Michael's untimely death on 25 June 2009 thwarted these grandiose plans. He collapsed at his rented mansion at 100 North Carolwood Drive in the Holmby Hills area of Los Angeles. He'd been in rehearsal for the O2 concerts, and in footage of his last rehearsal seemed to be in remarkably good shape and giving a flawless performance.

Nonetheless, the strain of the rehearsals appears to have contributed to a collapse and cardiac arrest, although some have alleged that he was administered with a large dose of Demerol shortly before he stopped breathing.

His personal physician, who was on the spot, attempted unsuccessfully to resuscitate him and made a 911 call for an ambulance at 12.22 am. Los Angeles Fire Department paramedics arrived at 12.35, but Michael was reportedly no longer breathing. Resuscitation efforts continued en route to the Ronald Reagan UCLA Medical Centre and for a further hour after his admission there.

Michael Jackson was finally pronounced dead at 2.25 am local time. One of the most colourful and controversial careers in the history of the entertainment industry had finally come to an end.

Celebrities pay tribute to **Michael Jackson**

"*My brother, the legendary king of pop, Michael Jackson, passed away on Thursday, June 25, at 2.26 pm... Our family requests that the media please respect our privacy during this tough time. May Allah be with you Michael, always.*"

JERMAINE JACKSON

THE MAN IN THE MIRROR Michael Jackson **59**

60 Michael Jackson **THE MAN IN THE MIRROR**

62 Michael Jackson **THE MAN IN THE MIRROR**

> **"** *I am absolutely devastated at this tragic and unexpected news. For Michael to be taken away from us so suddenly at such a young age, I just don't have the words.* **"**

QUINCY JONES

"I can't stop crying over the sad news. I have always admired Michael Jackson. The world has lost one of the greats, but his music will live on forever! My heart goes out to his three children and other members of his family. God bless."

MADONNA

"He was a wonderful man and will be greatly missed."

BRITNEY SPEARS

"I am heartbroken. My prayers go out to the Jackson family,and my heart goes out to his children. Let us remember him for his unparalleled contribution to the world of music, his generosity of spirit in his quest to heal the world & the joy he brought to his millions of devoted fans throughout the world. I feel blessed to have performed with him several times & to call him my friend. No artist will ever take his place. His star will shine forever."

MARIAH CAREY

"Michael Jackson showed me that you can actually see the beat. He made the music come to life!! He made me believe in magic. I will miss him."

P DIDDY

"Michael Jackson was one of the best that ever did it. RIP"

PINK

> *He was a kind, genuine and wonderful man. He was also one of the greatest entertainers that ever lived. I loved him very much and I will miss him every remaining day of my life.*

LIZA MINNELLI

"I'm shocked and devastated. I am hoping this is a dream I will wake up from, but it is not. Michael is dead. For him not to be around, that he's gone, is just surreal. It cannot sink into my psyche. He was a genius."

URI GELLER

"My heart is overcome with sadness for the devastating loss of my true friend Michael. He was an extraordinary friend, artist and contributor to the world. I join his family and his fans in celebrating his incredible life and mourning his untimely passing."

BROOKE SHIELDS

"When we worked together on Bad, I was in awe of his absolute mastery of movement on the one hand, and of the music on the other... He was wonderful to work with, an absolute professional at all times, and - it really goes without saying - a true artist. It will be a while before I can get used to the idea that he's no longer with us."

MARTIN SCORSESE

"Even though I met him, knew him, if I saw him on the streets I still would have been like 'Aaaah!'. He is just iconic on all levels. He was definitely the ultimate celebrity. Any celebrity who met Michael Jackson was completely (in) awe, I know I was."

SERENA WILLIAMS

> *I am so very sad and confused with every emotion possible... I am heartbroken for his children who I know were everything to him and for his family. This is such a massive loss on so many levels, words fail me.*

LISA MARIE PRESLEY

"I will be mourning my friend, brother, mentor and inspiration... He gave me and my family hope. I would never have been without him."

MC HAMMER

"Goodness. Michael Jackson. Poor old soul. Oh dear."

STEPHEN FRY

"We lost a great entertainer and a pop icon. My thoughts and prayers go out to Michael Jackson's family, friends and fans."

ARNOLD SCHWARZENEGGER

"We have lost a genius and a true ambassador of not only pop music, but of all music. He has been an inspiration to multiple generations, and I will always cherish the moments I shared with him onstage and all of the things I learned about music from him and the time we spent together."

JUSTIN TIMBERLAKE

"He was magic. He was what we all strive to be. He will always be the king of pop."

BEYONCE

"I am stunned. My friend Michael Jackson is dead. He lived with me for a week on 'Golden Pond' set after 'Thriller.'"

JANE FONDA

"Having a million different reactions I didn't expect I would feel... He was a great singer - God gives you certain gifts and this child was just an extraordinary child touched by this ability. He could sing like nobody else and he was able to connect with people."

CHER

"I am overwhelmed by this tragedy. Michael Jackson has been an idol for me all my life. He was not only a talented person but he was unique - a genius. It's such a loss. It feels like when Kennedy died, when Elvis died. My sympathy goes to the family. It's a big loss and it's not even sinking in right now."

CELINE DION

"Really sad news about Michael. He was talent from on high."

SLASH

"Just as there will never be another Fred Astaire or Chuck Berry or Elvis Presley, there will never be anyone comparable to Michael Jackson... His talent, his wonderment and his mystery make him legend."

STEVEN SPIELBERG

"NO OMG... Sending my love and prayers out to Michael and his family."

LINDSAY LOHAN

"Michael Jackson was easily as influential as James Brown, and that's saying a lot. He was the Fred Astaire of his time."

ALICE COOPER

"We are out of our joy. He is out of his pain. ... He was constantly challenged in the press and all he really wanted to be was the greatest entertainer and he was that."

REV. JESSE JACKSON

"Michael Jackson dying is absolutely devastating. I am totally shocked. MJ, you're the best."

PETER ANDRE

"When we worked together on 'Bad' I was in awe of his absolute mastery of movement on the one hand, and of the music on the other. Every step he took was absolutely precise and fluid at the same time. It was like watching quicksilver in motion."

WHITNEY HOUSTON

"He broke barriers, he changed radio formats. With music, he made it possible for people like Oprah Winfrey and Barack Obama to impact the mainstream world. His legacy is unparalleled."

USHER

"I feel privileged to have hung out and worked with Michael. He was a massively talented boy man with a gentle soul. His music will be remembered forever and my memories of our time together will be happy ones.

SIR PAUL McCARTNEY

"Michael was a friend and undoubtedly one of the world's greatest entertainers that I fortunately had the pleasure of working with. We have lost an icon in our industry."

DIONNE WARWICK

"He was a fun kid and did so much. He always reinvented himself time and time again and certainly was a great entertainer and dancer and great to watch with all that energy. He was excited about getting back to the stage."

JOE PESCI

"I was so excited to see his show in London. We were going to be on tour in Europe at the same time and I was going to fly in to see him. He has been an inspiration throughout my entire life and I'm devastated he's gone!"

BRITNEY SPEARS

"The last time we saw him he was in London a few weeks ago. He was absolutely fine. I can't believe this, it's such a shock. I'll always remember him as being a very sweet, kind and loving man."

MARK LESTER

"MJ was the best of the best. His music and performances made the world a brighter place. His light will shine on forever."

COLDPLAY

"Michael Jackson made culture accept a person of colour way before Tiger Woods, way before Oprah Winfrey, way before Barack Obama.Michael Jackson was a trailblazer. He was a historic figure that people will measure music and the industry by."

REVEREND AL SHARPTON

"You cannot say enough about what he has given to us musically and culturally. We take for granted people like him...all he wanted to do was give us great music and that's what he did. Every single day was dedicated to us. What a great time. What a great entertainer. There will never be anybody like him. Let's just honour that guy for all he's done."

JAMIE FOXX

"He felt pressure in every way. He has been under real scrutiny these last 10 or 15 years and in real financial trouble. I will mourn his loss, but I'm grateful that for a brief moment I got to stand on stage nightly and watch him sing and do those moves. He felt pressure in every way. He has been under real scrutiny these last 10 or 15 years and in real financial trouble. I will mourn his loss, but I'm grateful that for a brief moment I got to stand on stage nightly and watch him sing and do those moves."

SHERYL CROWE

"Oh my God."

KATY PERRY

"I got to work with Michael on a track that has not been released and it was the most amazing experience I've had in the studio. He was funny. Very funny and we laughed the whole time. I also saw what a beautiful father he was. He was a beautiful human being."

LENNY KRAVITZ

"Michael Jackson showed me that you can actually see the beat. He made the music come to life. He made me believe in magic. I will miss him."

P DIDDY

"Michael Jackson was my inspiration. Love and blessings."

MILEY CYRUS

"My heart, my mind are broken. I loved Michael with all my soul and I can't imagine life without him. We had so much in common and we had such loving fun together. I was packing up my clothes to go to London for his opening when I heard the news. I still can't believe it. I don't want to believe it. It can't be so. He will live in my heart forever but it's not enough. My life feels so empty. I don't think anyone knew how much we loved each other. The purest most giving love I've ever known. Oh God! I'm going to miss him. I can't yet imagine life without him. But I guess with God's help I'll learn. I keep looking at the photo he gave me of himself, which says, 'To my true love Elizabeth, I love you forever.' And, I will love HIM forever."

ELIZABETH TAYLOR

The albums, the songs and **the man himself**

The tragic death of Michael dominated the news for the entirety of June 2009. The sudden shock departure of a music legend led the world to think closely about the music and memories that Jackson left as a legacy to the world. Now one year on we will explore the albums and songs of Michael Jackson, looking at the critical receptions they received as well as some powerful lyrics and a string of number ones.

Michael Jackson defined pop music as it is today; his voice is instantly recognisable to any pop fan across the whole world. Jackson's title as King of Pop is more than just a title; many musicians of the genre name him as their primary inspiration and mentor throughout their early careers.

But why was Jackson so successful? Some claim that it was down to his unique style and passion for music, others that it was due to his innovative music videos and creative and memorable dance routines, others still for his eccentricity and peculiar habits. I would argue that all these things combined with his personality and undoubted talent led to the success and legend that is Michael Jackson.

Of course people often only remember Thriller,

I wrote a song called Dirty Diana. It was not about Lady Diana. It was about a certain kind of girls that hang around concerts or clubs, you know, they call them groupies.

released in 1982, in connection with Jackson. It was undoubtedly his biggest success and the album still holds the record to this day for most sales worldwide His other records, including Off The Wall (1979), Bad (1987), Dangerous (1991) and HIStory (1995), also rank among the world's best-selling.

Jackson is one of the few artists to have been inducted into the Rock and Roll Hall of Fame twice. Some of his other achievements include multiple Guinness World Records; 13 Grammy Awards (as well as the Grammy Legend Award and the Grammy Lifetime Achievement Award); 26 American Music Awards (more than any other artist, including the "Artist of the Century"); 13 number-one singles in the United States in his solo career (more than any other male artist in the Hot 100 era); and the estimated sale of over 800 million records worldwide. Jackson won hundreds of awards, which have made him the most-awarded recording artist in the history of music.

Got To Be There

1971

Released as Michael Jackson's first solo album, the album proved to be a reasonable success under the Motown Records label. It was released in 1971 and was generally well received by the critics.

The first single was the title track "Got To Be There" which was a Top 10 hit in both the US and the UK. The second single "Rockin Robin" hit the number 2 spot in the singles chart on both sides of the Atlantic. Different third singles were released in the US and UK, with the well-known Bill Withers hit "Ain't No Sunshine" making it a hat trick of Top 10 hits in the UK from the album.

Rolling Stone called the album "a slick, artful and every bit as good as the regular Jackson 5 product... a sweetly touching voice... innocence and utter professionalism... fascinating and finally irresistible."

ALBUM TRACK LISTINGS:

1. Ain't No Sunshine
2. I Wanna Be Where You Are
3. Girl Don't Take Your Love From Me
4. In Our Small Way
5. Got to Be There
6. Rockin' Robin
7. Wings of My Love
8. Maria (You Were the Only One)
9. Love Is Here and Now You're Gone
10. You've Got a Friend

> *If all the people in Hollywood who have had plastic surgery went on vacation, there wouldn't be a person left in town.*

Ben

RELEASED JANUARY 24, 1972

Ben' was Michael Jackson's second solo album with Motown Records. By this time Michael was already beginning to have frosty relationships with Motown; he felt that they weren't allowing him the freedom to create his own style. It was released in 1972 shortly after the Jackson 5 released their own album called 'Looking Through The Windows'. Only one single was released from the album, the title track 'Ben', which managed to sell over one million copies worldwide. The album itself was believed to have sold around five million copies worldwide.

Lindsay Planer of Allmusic said 'What Goes Around Comes Around' as being "one of Ben's better deep cuts" and 'Shoo Be Doo Be Doo Da Day' as being a "winner" while describing 'In Our Small Way' as being a "lesser note" for the album, having felt that the song contained a "hopelessly dated message"'.

ALBUM TRACK LISTINGS:

1. Ben
2. The Greatest Show On Earth
3. People Make The World Go Round
4. We've Got a Good Thing Going
5. Everybody's Somebody's Fool
6. My Girl
7. What Goes Around Comes Around
8. In Our Small Way
9. Shoo-Be-Doo-Be-Doo-Da-Day
10. You Can Cry On My Shoulder

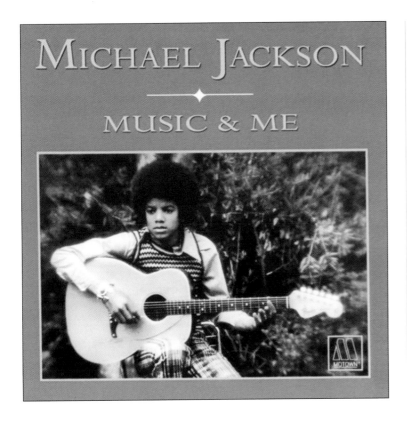

Music & Me

RELEASED AUGUST 1, 1972

This was the third solo album for Michael Jackson with Motown Records, all three of which were released with 15 months.

Michael was now 14 years old and his voice was beginning to change on this album. It was also the start of the time when Michael was beginning to want more input into his music in terms of playing instruments and contributing to some of the song writing. However Motown would not allow Michael to express any of this creativity. As mentioned previously the relationship between Jackson and the record company had become sour and this turned out to be his penultimate release with the label. Michael had started to develop a fan base and his own unique style and voice.

The album was a flop largely due to the label's decision not to promote the albums tracks. It barely troubled the charts and sold roughly one million copies worldwide.

ALBUM TRACK LISTINGS:

1. With A Child's Heart
2. Up Again
3. All The Things You Are
4. Happy (a theme from Lady Sings The Blues)
5. Too Young
6. Doggin' Around
7. Johnny Raven
8. Euphoria
9. Morning Glow
10. Music and Me

Forever, Michael

RELEASED JANUARY 1, 1975

Interestingly, unlike his previous three albums which were released within a 15 month period, Jackson's fans had to wait almost two years for this album to be released and it showed the signs of a complete breakdown between Motown Records and Jackson. Michael was now 16 and his voice and singing style had changed since his earliest Motown recordings. The album became his last release with Motown.

Only two singles were originally released in the U.S with 'Just A Little Bit of You' making the Top 30. In 1981, in a bid to capitalise on Michael's new found solo success after leaving Motown Records and releasing the smash hit album 'Off The Wall', Motown put together various Michael and Jackson 5 recordings including the album track 'One Day In Your Life'. They also named the album 'One Day In Your Life' as well as releasing it as a single where it went on to hit number one in the UK and become one of the biggest hits of the year.

ALBUM TRACK LISTINGS:

1. We're Almost There
2. Take Me Back
3. One Day In Your Life
4. Cinderella Stay Awhile
5. We've Got Forever
6. Just A Little Bit Of You
7. You Are There
8. Dapper Dan
9. Dear Michael
10. I'll Come Home To You

Off The Wall

RELEASED AUGUST 10, 1979

Off The Wall' was arguably the breakthrough album for Michael Jackson signalling his move away from the Jackson 5 and developing his own style and musical taste. This album also began the close relationship with Quincy Jones, who is credited with being the brains behind Michael's talent. Recording sessions took place between December 1978 and June 1979 at Allen Zentz Recording, Westlake Recording Studios, and Cherokee Studios in Los Angeles, California. Jackson collaborated with a number of other writers and performers such as Paul McCartney, Stevie Wonder and Rod Temperton. Jackson wrote several of the songs himself, including the Platinum-certified lead single, 'Don't Stop 'Til You Get Enough'.

The record was a departure from Jackson's previous work for Motown. Several critics observed that 'Off The Wall' was crafted from funk, disco-pop, soul, soft rock, jazz and pop ballads. Jackson received positive reviews for his vocal performance on the record. The record gained positive reviews and won the singer his first Grammy Award since the early 1970s. With 'Off The Wall', Jackson became the first solo artist to have four singles from the same album peak inside the top 10 of the Billboard Hot 100. The album was a commercial success, to date it is certified for eight Multi-Platinum discs in the US and has sold more than 20 million copies worldwide.

DON'T STOP 'TIL YOU GET ENOUGH

The lead track for the album, 'Don't Stop 'Til You Get Enough', is regarded as one of Jackson's most memorable hits to this day. At over six minutes long it breaks the traditional rules of popular music where songs should be roughly three to four minutes in length. It was Jackson's first solo number one in the United States Billboard 100 chart. It is considered by most critics to be Jackson's first chance to showcase his talents not only as a singer but also a writer and performer. Stephen Holden, of Rolling Stone, described the song as "one of a handful of recent disco releases that works both as a dance track and as an aural extravaganza comparable to Earth, Wind and Fire's 'Boogie Wonderland.'"

Jason Elias, a writer for All music, noted that 'Don't Stop 'Til You Get Enough' presents a "new Michael Jackson" that was "sexual, adult, and aggressive. Like the best of Jones' late-'70s, early-'80s work, this song wasn't quite disco, couldn't be hardcore funk - it was an amalgam of styles with the all-important pop accessibility."

ROCK WITH YOU

The second song from the 'Off The Wall' breakthrough album, 'Rock With You' was almost as successful as 'Don't Stop 'Til You Get Enough'. The song was collaboration between Jackson and Rod Templeton who would later go on to write 'Thriller' with Jackson. The song is regarded by many as the last great song of the disco era

of music. It reached number one of both the pop and R and B charts in the United States. Jackson once said in an interview that it was one of his personal favourite songs. The song has since been covered by a variety of artists from Chris Brown to Jackson's own sister Janet.

WORKING DAY AND NIGHT

A relatively unknown song from the album. The song symbolises Jackson's fusion of both disco and pop music. Some critics have said the song should be more memorable than it actual is due to its genius and catchy rhythm.

GET ON THE FLOOR

Written as collaboration between Jackson and Louis Johnson a session bass guitarist who also worked on 'Thriller', 'Get On The Floor' is a popular track with the diehard fans of Jackson. One critic from All music said "although everyone knows the classic Jackson songs, only the diehards know songs like 'Get On The Floor', which is a shame because it is in my opinion better than 'Thriller.'"

OFF THE WALL

The title track of the album and again co-written with Rod Temperton the song was less successful than the album title itself. It peaked at number 5 in the American singles chart. It was later sampled in 2008 by Mariah

Carey. However it was Jackson's third successful top 10 single to come from the album.

GIRLFRIEND

The song was written by Paul McCartney and he thought it was perfectly suited to Michael Jackson. When Jones suggested the song to Jackson he was unaware that McCartney had written it specifically for him. However the song performed very badly charting only at number 41.

SHE'S OUT OF MY LIFE

This song was originally written about the life of Karen Carpenter by the musician Tom Bahler who had recently split up with her. In the video for the song Jackson breaks down into tears at the end as he sings the word "life". The song became a key part of Jackson live show set for years. The song peaked at number 10 in the USA but reached as high as number 3 in the UK.

The other songs on the album are less well known they are 'I Can't Help It', 'It's The Falling In Love' and 'Burn This Disco Out'.

Thriller
RELEASED NOVEMBER 30, 1982

Thriller' is the most famous album of all time and the record breaking seller worldwide. If you ask anyone about Michael Jackson the first thing that comes to mind is either the moonwalk or 'Thriller'. Recording sessions took place between April and November 1982 at Westlake Recording

> *Our parents taught us to always be respectful and, no matter what you do, to give it everything you have. Be the best, not the second best.*
>
> USA TODAY 2001

Studios in Los Angeles, California, with a production budget of $750,000. Assisted by producer Quincy Jones, Jackson wrote four of 'Thriller's' nine tracks. In just over a year, 'Thriller' became and currently remains the best-selling album of all time, with sales estimated by various sources as somewhere between 75 and 110 million copies worldwide. Seven of the album's nine songs were released as singles, and all reached the top 10 on the Billboard Hot 100. The album won a record-breaking eight Grammy Awards at the 1984 Grammys.

'Thriller' cemented Jackson's status as one of the pre-eminent pop stars of the late 20th century, and enabled him to break down racial barriers via his appearances on MTV and meeting with President Ronald Reagan at the White House. The album was one of the first to use music videos as successful promotional tools and the videos for 'Thriller', 'Billie Jean' and 'Beat It' all received regular rotation on MTV, and still do to this day.

WANNA BE STARTIN' SOMETHIN'

It was released as the fourth single from the 'Thriller' album but is the first song on the album itself. The song was written by Jackson and produced by Quincy Jones. The song's lyrics pertain to strangers spreading rumours to begin or start an argument just for no reason. Musically, 'Wanna Be Startin' Somethin' has a cross-cultural disco theme, similar to Jackson's material from 'Off The Wall' in 1979. The song's rhythm arrangement consists of interweaving drum-machine patterns, while the horn arrangement is brassy and precise.

'Wanna Be Startin' Somethin' was generally well received by contemporary music critics. The song was also commercially successful, charting within the top twenty and top thirty in multiple countries. The song became Jackson's fifth consecutive top ten single in the United States on the Billboard Hot 100, peaking within the top ten at number five.

THE GIRL IS MINE

This song was another collaboration between Jackson and Paul McCartney and was released as the first single from the 'Thriller' album. Some of the public were not impressed by 'The Girl Is Mine', as they felt that Jackson and Jones had created a song for the white pop audience whereas their traditional fan base had been the Black American public.

Despite this, 'The Girl Is Mine' achieved success in the

music charts. Aside from topping the R&B singles chart, the single peaked at number two on the Billboard Hot 100 and number eight in the UK. By 1985, it had sold 1.3 million copies, and was eventually certified platinum. Interestingly many critics thought that 'Thriller' itself would be a huge disappointment on the back of this single with one saying that Jackson "had sold out."

THRILLER

Some would argue that this is Jackson's most famous song of all time but not necessarily for the music. 'Thriller' was voted the best music video of all time by both MTV and Rolling Stone Magazine for its innovative movie like qualities. Quincy Jones again worked with Jackson on the record which was the seventh and final single released from the album.

Musically 'Thriller' is a pop rock song; the song's instruments include a bassline and synthesizer. In the song, sound effects such as a creaking door, thunder, feet walking on wooden planks, winds and howling dogs can be heard, and the lyrics contain frightening themes and elements. 'Thriller' received positive reviews from critics, though the song was outshone by its music video. 'Thriller' became Jackson's seventh top-ten single from the album.

However it is the video that's more famous than the song, at fourteen minutes the video is substantially longer than the song, which ties together a narrative

> *And my goal in life is to give to the world what I was lucky to receive: the ecstasy of divine union through my music and my dance.*

featuring Jackson and actress Ola Ray in a setting heavily inspired by horror films of the 1950s. In the video's most iconic scene, Jackson leads other actors costumed as zombies in a choreographed dance routine.

Though it garnered some criticism for its occult theme and violent imagery, the video was immediately popular and received high critical acclaim, being nominated for six MTV Video Music Awards in 1984 and winning three. Ashley Lasimone noted that 'Thriller' "became a signature for Jackson" and described "the

> *When you just look out over the stage, as far as the naked eye could see, you see people. And it's a wonderful feeling, but it came with a lot of pain, a lot of pain.*

EBONY MAGAZINE 2008

> *"Yeah, Wacko Jacko, where did that come from? Some English tabloid. I have a heart and I have feelings. I feel that when you do that to me. It's not nice."*

groove of its bassline, paired with Michael's killer vocals and sleek moves" as having had "produced a frighteningly great single."

BEAT IT

'Beat It' from the album 'Thriller' is one of the best known of Jackson's singles. The song was very popular with both critics and fans alike. It was the third single released from the Thriller album. 'Beat It' was awarded two Grammy Awards and two American Music Awards and was inducted into the Music Video Producers Hall of Fame. Rolling Stone magazine placed 'Beat It' in the 337th spot on its list of The 500 Greatest Songs of All Time.

In a Rolling Stone review, Christopher Connelly describes 'Beat It' as the best song on 'Thriller', adding that it "ain't no disco AOR track". He notes of the "nifty dance song", "Jackson's voice soars all over the melody, Eddie Van Halen checks in with a blistering guitar solo, you could build a convention centre on the backbeat".

The song reached number one on the American singles chart but only number 3 in the UK singles chart.

BILLIE JEAN

It was written by Jackson and produced by Quincy Jones for the singer's sixth solo album, 'Thriller'. Originally disliked by Jones, the track was almost removed from the album after he and Jackson had disagreements regarding it.

There are contradictory claims to what the song's lyrics refer to. Some people believe that they are derived from a real-life experience, in which a mentally ill female fan claimed that Jackson had fathered one of her twins. Others believed that the song was about tennis great Billie Jean King. Jackson was an avid tennis fan. Jackson himself, however, stated that 'Billie Jean' was based on groupies he had encountered. The song reached number one in both the US and the UK.

The song was reworked for a Pepsi commercial just a

year or so later, in which Jackson premiered it at the Grammy Awards which he later collected a record eight awards.

HUMAN NATURE

The song was written by Steve Pocarro and John Betis especially for Jackson's vocals. Released as the fifth single from the album, it performed reasonably well reaching number 2 in the US. However the song was never released as a single in the UK until after his death in 2009 where it reached number 62.

PRETTY YOUNG THING

Often abbreviated as PYT, 'Pretty Young Thing' was a cover of an original song by Greg Phillinganes. Released as the sixth single from the album it was perhaps the least well received of the 'Thriller' album except for the 'Girl is Mine'. It only reached number 10 in the US Chart. Rolling Stone reviewer Christopher Connelly, while discussing the album in a review, stated that the song "isn't up to the spunky character of the other tracks." Connelly mentioned that one of Jackson's weaknesses was "a tendency to go for the glitz," and cited the song as one example of this

The other songs on the album were less well known; they included 'The Lady In My Life' and 'Baby Be Mine'.

Bad
RELEASED OCTOBER 1, 1987

The album was released on August 31, 1987 by Epic/CBS Records, nearly five years after Jackson's previous studio album, 'Thriller', which went on to become the world's best-selling album. 'Bad' itself sold over 30 million copies worldwide, and shipped eight million units in the

United States alone, and has been cited as being one of the bestselling albums of all time. 'Bad' is the only album to have five of its singles peak at number one on the Billboard Hot 100. Similar to Jackson's previous music material, the album's music features elements of R&B, pop and rock.

'Bad' was recorded throughout 1987. The lyrical themes on the record relate to paranoia, romance and self-improvement. 'Bad' is widely regarded as having cemented Jackson's status as one of the most successful artists of the 1980s, as well enhancing his solo career and being one of the best musical projects of his career. Despite the album's commercial success, it has been viewed as a relative failure when compared to the sales of 'Thriller'.

Ten of the eleven songs on 'Bad' were released as singles; one was a promotional single and another was released outside of the United States and Canada. One of the singles charted within the top-ten, and another charted within the top-twenty on the Hot 100. The single that was released outside of the United States and Canada was commercially successful, charting within the top ten and top twenty in multiple territories. 'Bad' peaked at number one in seven countries, as well as charting within the top twenty in other territories.

'Bad' was generally well received although some critics noted that 'Bad' did not measure up to the success of 'Thriller'. Davitt Sigerson, of Rolling Stone, stated that "even without a milestone recording like 'Billie Jean', 'Bad' is still a better record than 'Thriller', just not in the terms of sales and financial gains."

BAD

Despite being the title track 'Bad' was actually the second single released from the album after 'I Just Can't Stop Loving You'. It is regarded as one of the most popular songs from the entirety of Michael Jackson's catalogue. 'Bad' was originally intended to be a duet between Jackson and musician Prince; although the plans were not followed-up on. In Jackson's 1988 autobiography 'Moonwalk', Jackson discussed the concept of 'Bad', elaborating that, "'Bad' is a song about the street. It's about this kid from a bad neighbourhood who gets to go away to a private school. He comes back to the old neighbourhood when he's on a break from school and the kids from the neighbourhood start giving him trouble. He sings, 'I'm bad, you're bad, who's bad, who's the best?' He's saying when you're strong and good, and then you're bad."

Some critics noted that 'Bad' helped Jackson's image become edgier during the 'Bad'-era of popular music where the public preferred edgier artists. The song peaked at number one on the Billboard Hot 100, and remained at the top position of the chart for two weeks, becoming Jackson's 'Bad' album's second number one single, and Jackson's seventh number one entry on the chart. It also charted at number one in the United Kingdom.

THE WAY YOU MAKE ME FEEL

It was the third single from Jackson's seventh studio album 'Bad'. Written by Jackson and produced by Jackson and Quincy Jones, the song is credited as being a pop and R&B song. The lyrics pertain to being in love with someone. Aside from appearing on Jackson's 'Bad' album, the song has also been featured on the first disc of Jackson's complication album 'HIStory: Past, Present and Future, Book I' in 1995 and 'This Is It' in 2009. 'The Way You Make Me Feel' has been covered by multiple recording artists since its release.

The song received positive reviews from contemporary critics. 'The Way You Make Me Feel' became 'Bad's' third consecutive single to peak at number one on Billboard's Hot 100 music chart, and charted mainly within the top ten and twenty internationally.

LIBERIAN GIRL

The 9th single to be released from the album 'Liberian Girl' was actually written back in 1983. It only reached number 13 in the United Kingdom. However the song is better known for its music video than the actual song. The video featured Whoopi Goldberg, Quincy Jones, Jackie Collins, John Travolta, Olivia Newton John, Steven Spielberg and David Copperfield.

ANOTHER PART OF ME

Produced by Jackson and Quincy Jones for the singer's seventh solo album, 'Bad', the song was originally featured in Jackson's 1986 3-D film Captain EO. It was later released as the record's sixth single on July 11, 1988 and appeared as a dance attack and level song for the Michael Jackson's Moonwalker video game. The lyrics emphasize global unity, love, outreach and possible religious themes.

MAN IN THE MIRROR

Voted the favourite song of Jackson's fans in a 2009 poll taken after his death. It peaked at number one in the United States when released as a single in early 1988 off his seventh solo album, 'Bad'. It is one of Jackson's most critically acclaimed songs and it was nominated for Record of the Year at the Grammy Awards. The song topped the Billboard Hot 100 for two weeks. It was only a moderate hit in the UK at the time of its release, peaking at number 21 and becoming the only single from 'Bad' not to reach the UK Top 20 on first release. However, in 2009, following the news of Jackson's death, the song peaked at number two in the official UK

Singles Chart.

Richard Corliss, writing in Time Magazine in 2009, described the song as "toweringly indulgent but well-meaning", praising it as one of Jackson's most powerful vocal performances and "accessible social statements" as well as noting its "fleeting glimpse of autobiography."

I JUST CAN'T STOP LOVING YOU

The song is a popular ballad by singer Michael Jackson featuring a duet with Siedah Garrett. Written and composed by Jackson, it was originally intended to be a duet between Jackson and his woman of choice: either Barbra Streisand or Whitney Houston. Even Aretha Franklin and Agnetha Fältskog (formerly of ABBA) were offered the song, but all four had other obligations. It was the first song released from the 'Bad' album. The song became the first of five consecutive number-one Billboard Hot 100 singles from Jackson's 'Bad' album. It also reached number one on the Billboard R&B and adult contemporary charts.

DIRTY DIANA

The fifth single from the album, 'Dirty Diana' was fairly well received by the music critics of the era. The song achieved worldwide success charting at number one in the USA and the top 10 almost everywhere else worldwide. Davitt Sigerson of Rolling Stone gave the

> *Actually, I am one of the loneliest people on this earth. I cry sometimes, because it hurts. It does. To be honest, I guess you could say that it hurts to be me.*

song a more positive review, though calling it a "filler", she still commented that the song, along with "Speed Demon" is what makes 'Bad' "richer, sexier, better than Thriller's forgettable songs."

SMOOTH CRIMINAL

'Smooth Criminal' was a song that almost didn't make it into the 'Bad' album. With the final decision to include

And I remember going to the record studio and there was a park across the street and I'd see all the children playing and I would cry because it would make me sad that I would have to work instead.

the song, Jackson originally decided to make the music video a western-styled short film. However, he later decided to change the style into a 1930s nightclub style. An early version of the song was written by Jackson and John Barnes in 1985 and the original demo was recorded in 1986. The original title was 'Al Capone'. This version didn't make the album and was re-worked and re-written as 'Smooth Criminal'. The song reached number 7 in the USA and number 3 in the UK, one of the more disappointing single performances from the 'Bad' album releases. The song was later covered by Alien Ant Farm in 2001.

LEAVE ME ALONE

The song was the eighth release from the album but wasn't released in the US or Canada. The song peaked at number one in the United Kingdom. 'Leave Me Alone' was generally well received by contemporary music critics. Stephen Thomas Erlewine, a writer for Allmusic, stated he felt that 'Leave Me Alone' was the best track on Bad, commenting "why are all of his best songs paranoid anthems?"

Other songs on the album include 'Speed Demon' and 'Just good Friends'. The album also featured several interviews with Quincy Jones and hidden bonus tracks like 'Streetwalker'.

Dangerous
RELEASED JANUARY 1, 1991

Dangerous' became Jackson's second album to debut at number one in the American Billboard Album Chart. The album has sold over 32 million copies worldwide since its release in 1991. The album managed to win a Grammy but the album wasn't entirely well received. 'Dangerous' was however the fastest selling album ever in the USA. The album also debuted at number one in the UK outselling U2's album 'Achtung Baby'.

JAM

The opening track of the 'Dangerous' album, the music video of the song famously featured basketball legend Michael Jordan. It peaked at number 26 in the USA and number 12 in the UK.

IN THE CLOSET

The song reached number 6 in the American charts. The song, written by Jackson and Teddy Riley, is about keeping a relationship secret between lovers. "In the closet" is an English idiom used when one is not open about an aspect of their life, particularly in regard to sexual orientation. Despite the song's suggestive name its lyrics do not allude to hidden sexual orientation but rather a concealed relationship; "Don't hide our love/ Woman to man." The New York Times stated, "Only Jackson would use that title for a heterosexual love song."

REMEMBER THE TIME

'Remember The Time' was generally well received by contemporary critics. The song was commercially successful, peaking at number three on the Billboard Hot 100 singles chart and number one on Billboard's R&B singles chart. The video features Eddie Murphy and Magic Johnson. Alan Light, a writer for Rolling Stone, stated that he felt 'Remember The Time' was the "most light-hearted musical track on the album," and described the song's lyrics as telling of a "blissful romance only to ask, 'So why did it end?'"

HEAL THE WORLD

'Heal the World' is a song from Michael Jackson's hit album, 'Dangerous', released in 1991. The music video features children living in countries suffering from unrest especially Burundi. It is also one of only a handful of Michael Jackson's videos not to feature Jackson himself, the others being 'Cry', 'HIStory' and 'Man in the Mirror'. Jackson performed the song in the Super Bowl XXVII halftime show with a 35,000 person flash card performance.

In a 2001 Internet chat with fans, Jackson said 'Heal the World' is the song he is most proud to have created. He also created the Heal the World Foundation, a charitable organization which was designed to improve the lives of children. The organization was also meant to teach children how to help others. This concept of 'betterment for all' would become a centrepiece for the Dangerous World Tour.

BLACK OR WHITE

The lead song from the album and undoubtedly the most popular and bestselling single from the album. The

100 Michael Jackson **THE MAN IN THE MIRROR**

To live is to be musical, starting with the blood dancing in your veins. Everything living has a rhythm. Do you feel your music?

song was the bestselling single of 1991 and peaked at number one in the charts. The song is often viewed as an attack on Jackson's critics talking about his perceived change of skin colour. Anti-racism campaigners have often used the lyrics as a campaign song and crediting Jackson for his work in this area.

DANGEROUS

The title track from the album, 'Dangerous' was the tenth single from the album. Prior to the planned release of the song, 'Dangerous' received a positive reaction from contemporary critics in reviews of the track's parent album. Jon Pareles, a writer for The New York Times, called it "his latest song about a predatory lover" and highlighted the lyrics "I felt taken by lust's strange inhumanity", observing, "He is a great dancer, yet his songs proclaim a terror of the body and of fleshly pleasures".

Other tracks from the album included 'Why you Wanna Trip On Me', 'She Drives Me Wild', 'Can't Let Her Get Away' and 'Keep The Faith'.

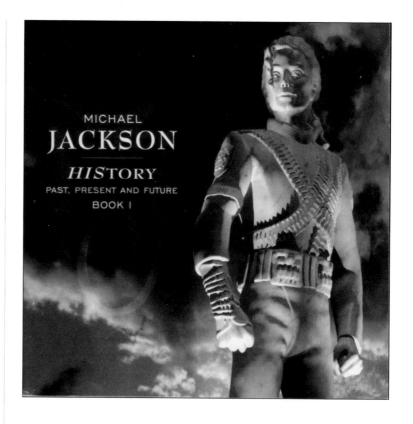

HIStory Past, Present and Future - Book 1

RELEASED JUNE 1, 1995

Jackson's first compilation album he ever released was taken from the biggest hits and songs from 'Thriller', 'Off The Wall', 'Bad' and 'Dangerous'. It was a worldwide success. 'HIStory' is primarily directed at the tabloid press. Starting in the late 1980s, Jackson and the press had a difficult relationship. In 1986, the tabloids ran a story claiming that Jackson slept in a hyperbaric oxygen chamber, which Jackson claimed was untrue. It was reported that Jackson had offered to buy the bones of Joseph Merrick (the "elephant man"). Jackson described the story "a complete lie". These stories inspired the pejorative nickname "Wacko Jacko", which Jackson despised.

In 1993, the relationship between Jackson and the press soured entirely when he was accused of child sexual abuse. Although he was not charged with a crime at the time, Jackson was subject to intense media scrutiny while the criminal investigation took place. The coverage was very controversial and constantly implied that he was guilty of the charges.

In 1994, Jackson said of the media coverage, "I will say I am particularly upset by the handling of the matter by the incredible, terrible mass media. At every opportunity, the media has dissected and manipulated these allegations to reach their own conclusions."

The album was recorded from September 1994 to March 1995. Jackson co-wrote and co-produced a majority of the songs featured on the album. Aside from Jackson, other writes include Dallas Austin, The Notorious B.I.G., Bruce Swedien, R. Kelly and Rene Moore and other producers include David Foster and Bill Bottrell. The album sold very well worldwide reaching number one in both the United Kingdom and the United States. 'HIStory' received generally positive reviews. Arguably Jackson's most angry and raw, emotional album, it revealed a musician worn, torn and possibly paranoid by years of superstardom, now reportedly reacting against people who tried to bring him down.

It also featured some new tracks notably 'Earth Song', 'You are Not Alone', 'They Don't Care About Us' and 'Stranger In Moscow' which I will now discuss in greater depth.

EARTH SONG

'Earth Song' is the third single from Michael Jackson's album 'HIStory'. It is a ballad that incorporates elements of blues, gospel and opera. Jackson had a long-standing history of releasing socially conscious material such as 'We Are the World', 'Man in the Mirror' and 'Heal the World'. However, 'Earth Song' was the first that overtly dealt with the environment and animal welfare. The song itself highlights Jackson's charitable nature and the humanitarian work he has achieved throughout his life. It received a Grammy nomination in 1997.

YOU ARE NOT ALONE

Originally written by R Kelly this moved Jackson closer to the R & B scene where his music arguably originated. The vast majority of critical reaction to 'You Are Not Alone' was positive, although it did not attain unanimous praise. The song was the recipient of Grammy and American Music Award nominations. The corresponding music video, which featured Jackson and his wife, was also notable for its scenes of semi-nudity. Commercially, the song was a significant success. It holds a Guinness World Record as the first song in the 37-year history of the Billboard Hot 100 to debut at number one.

THEY DON'T CARE ABOUT US

The song remains one of the most controversial pieces Jackson ever composed. In the US, media scrutiny surrounding alleged anti-Semitic lyrics were the catalyst for Jackson issuing multiple apologies and re-recording the album—altering the lyrics for that particular track. The singer countered allegations of anti-Semitism, arguing that reviews had misinterpreted the context of the song, either unintentionally or deliberately. Musically, it is an aggressive hip-hop production about social ills. Despite the song being a hit in Europe, it didn't perform well in the USA due in part to radio stations being reluctant to play the controversial song.

STRANGER IN MOSCOW

During his visit to Moscow in September, Jackson came up with the song 'Stranger in Moscow' which would be released on his 1995 album 'HIStory'. It was during a time when Jackson felt very alone, far away from his family and friends, yet every night throughout his tours fans would stay by his hotel and support him. 'Stranger in Moscow' turned out to be one of Jackson's most critically acclaimed songs ever.

James Hunter of Rolling Stone commented He is clearly angry, miserable, tortured, inflammatory, furious about what he calls, in 'Stranger in Moscow', a 'swift and sudden fall from grace'... 'HIStory' feels like the work of someone with a bad case of 'Thriller' nostalgia. Occasionally this backward focus works to Jackson's advantage.

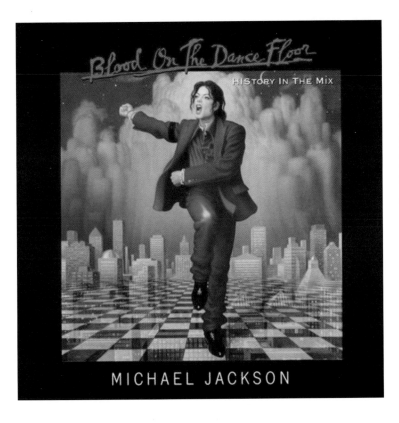

Blood on the Dance Floor / HIStory in the Mix

RELEASED MAY 1, 1997

The album 'Blood On The Dance Floor' was technically Jackson's eighth studio album released in 1997. This album mainly featured reworked tracks from the 'HIStory' album but also featured five new songs for fans to savour. It was designed to be a remix album of 'HIStory' combining the unique styles of Jackson's music with a modern twist. The album received minimal promotion by Jackson's standards, particularly in the US. Reviews at the time of release were largely mixed; some critics felt that Jackson had already explored these musical themes while others criticized what they perceived as weak vocals. Other critics were favourable, with praise issued for similarities to the music of Marilyn Manson and Trent Reznor.

Worldwide sales stand at six million copies as of 2010, making it the bestselling remix album ever released. Several contemporary critics view the material in an increasingly favourable light and believe the album could have been more successful—commentators argue that certain sections of the world took interest in tabloid stories about the singers' personal life over his musical career.

We have to heal our wounded world. The chaos, despair, and senseless destruction we see today are a result of the alienation that people feel from each other and their environment.

The new tracks for the album were 'Blood On Tthe Dancefloor', 'Morphine', 'Superfly Sister', 'Ghosts' and 'Is it Scary' although only 'Blood on the Dancefloor', 'Ghosts' and 'Is it Scary' had any success.

BLOOD ON THE DANCE FLOOR

Released as the first single from the album, it was originally intended to be use on the 1991 album 'Dangerous' but Jackson decided to save it for later. It was co-written by Jackson and Teddy Riley. The song is about a predatory woman by the name of Susie, who seduces Jackson before plotting to stab him with a knife. The composition explores a variety of genres ranging from rock to funk.

Commentators have compared the work, music and lyrics of 'Blood On The Dance Floor' to the music from 'Dangerous' saying that it was clear that Jackson had originally intended it to be released in 1991. The lead single peaked at number one in several countries, including the UK but only peaked at number 42 in the US Billboard 100.

MORPHINE

Written by Michael Jackson, the song was six and a half minutes long and criticised by critics for being uninteresting and too long. The song wasn't released as a single and isn't particularly well remembered by fans.

SUPERFLY SISTER

A collaboration between Jackson and Bryan Loren, the established music writer. The song wasn't released as a single from the album.

GHOSTS

'Ghosts' was written, composed and produced by Michael Jackson and Teddy Riley in 1997. A double A side was a remix of the 1995 song 'HIStory' and was remixed by legendary producer Tony Moran. Commentators made observations about the paranoid lyrics, a common theme in Jackson's work. The double A-side was promoted with a music video for each song. 'HIStory' was set in a nightclub, in a futuristic era, and recalled Jackson's filmography. 'Ghosts' was a five minute clip taken from the much longer film of the same name. The song would become a top five hit in the UK, but did not chart as highly elsewhere.

IS IT SCARY

'Is It Scary' is a song by American recording artist Michael Jackson. The song was originally written to have been featured in the 1993 film 'Addams Family Values', but the plans were cancelled after contract conflicts.

'Is It Scary' received mixed reviews from contemporary music critics. Musically, the song was viewed by music critics as showing a "darker side" of Jackson, and compared the songs composition to material from Marilyn Manson. In November 1997, a radio edit version of the song was released as a promotional single in the Netherlands, while promo singles containing remixes were released in the United States and the United Kingdom.

'Is It Scary' generally received positive to mixed reviews from contemporary music critics. Jim Farber, writer for the New York Daily News, commented that "'Is It Scary' boasts a few innovative sounds but no real melodies".

The other tracks from the album include the following remixes from the 'HIStory' album:

Track 5. Scream Louder - Flyte Time Remix

Track 6. Money - Fire Island Radio Edit

Track 7. 2 Bad - Refugee Camp Mix

Track 8. Stranger In Moscow - Tee's In-House Club Mix

Track 9. This Time Around - D.M Radio Mix

Track 10. Earth Song - Hani's Club Experience

Track 11. You Are Not Alone - Classic Club Mix

Track 12. History - Tony Moran's History Lesson

Invincible

2001

This was probably Jackson's worst ever received album with critics giving it a very mixed reception. Despite featuring 16 tracks only 4 ever became singles of any note. Those singles were 'Unbreakable', 'You Rock My World', 'Butterflies' and 'Speechless'. A recurring element from music critics

was that some felt that 'Invincible' was one of Jackson's least impressive records, mostly because of its length.

James Hunter, a writer for Rolling Stone, gave 'Invincible' three out of five stars, generally praising the album's songs, but noted that the album's later ballads made the record too long. Hunter also commented that Jackson and Riley made 'Invincible' "something really handsome and smart", allowing listeners "to concentrate on the track's momentous rhythms" such as Santana's passionate interjections and Lubbock's wonderfully arranged symphonic sweeps".

Despite the mixed reception however, the album reached number one in the Billboard album charts and in the UK album chart. 'Invincible' re-entered music charts several times during the decade, despite the reported worldwide sales of thirteen million copies, but although sales were reasonable the album has been viewed as a commercial failure compared to Jackson's previous albums sales.

UNBREAKABLE

This featured the Notorious BIG on vocals. However like the album as a whole it was critically disappointing with most people calling it the last album of a desperate Jackson. The song was a medium hit worldwide charting in the top 20 in both the United States and the United Kingdom

YOU ROCK MY WORLD

The song was released as the lead single from the album in August 2001 by Epic Records. The lyrics pertain to being in love and trying to gain a female's affection. The song is musically a disco pop song with influences from Jackson's' songs from his previous studio albums with Quincy Jones.

The song received mixed reviews from music critics, with reviewers commenting that Jackson could have made a better effort for the song and that the song was not his best material, while other reviewers generally praising the song's composition and Jackson's vocal performance.

The song peaked at number ten on the Billboard Hot 100, becoming Jackson's first top ten single in the United States in over six years, and his last top ten single in the country for the remainder of his career.

BUTTERFLIES

It was written by Marsha Ambrosius and Andre Harris, and produced by Jackson and Harris. The track appears on Jackson's tenth, and final, studio album, 'Invincible' (2001). 'Butterflies' is a mid tempo ballad song with R&B musical styles. The single received generally mixed reviews from music critics; some music reviewers described the song as being one of the best song's on Invincible while others felt that it was a "decent track".

> *When I step out on stage in front of thousands of people, I don't feel that I'm being brave. It can take much more courage to express true feelings to one person. In spite of the risks, the courage to be honest and intimate opens the way to self-discovery.*

SPEECHLESS

'Speechless' is a song by the American recording artist Michael Jackson, included on his tenth studio album, 'Invincible' (2001). The singer was inspired to write the ballad after a water balloon fight with youngsters in Germany. Andrae Crouch and his gospel choir provided backing vocals. Executives at Jackson's record label, Epic Records, responded positively to the track when given a preview several months before 'Invincible's' release. 'Speechless' was issued as a promotional single, receiving mixed reviews from music critics. Commentary focused on the track's a cappellas, lyrics and music. Some called it an original triumph for Jackson but other argued that it sounded dated and dull.

What has happened since Michael's death

Michael Jackson was found unconscious on June 25th 2009. Now just over a year on, we are going to look back on what is now known about that fateful night where one of the biggest music legends of the modern era passed away. His personal physician Conrad Murray who tried to resuscitate Jackson on the night was later arrested and charged with the crime of manslaughter, Jackson was administered a cocktail of drugs on the nights and the offices of Conrad Murray were searched.

The coroner ruled that Jackson's death was ultimately homicide and that there should be an investigation into his death. On February 8, 2010, Murray pleaded not guilty to charges of involuntary manslaughter, and was released from prison after posting a US$75,000 bail.

Jackson's death triggered an outpouring of grief around the world, creating unprecedented surges of internet traffic and causing sales of his music and that of the Jackson 5 to increase dramatically. Jackson had been scheduled to perform his 'This Is It' concert series to over one million people at London's O2 arena, from July 13, 2009 to March 6, 2010.

His public memorial service was held on July 7, 2009, at the Staples Center in Los Angeles, where he had rehearsed for the London concerts the night before his death. His memorial service was broadcast live around the world, attracting a global audience of up to one billion people.

Latoya Jackson has repeatedly stated her believe that Jackson was murdered because as she said "he was

> ## I just wanted to say that these will be my final show performances in London.
> ## When I say this is it, it really means this is it.

worth more to people dead than alive, his money was all available once he died" After Murray pleaded not guilty to the manslaughter charge, several members of the Jackson family said they felt he deserved a more severe charge. On June 25, 2010, the last date they could serve a notice on Murray, Joseph Jackson filed a wrongful death lawsuit against Jackson's personal physician. The lawsuit alleges that Murray repeatedly lied to cover up his use of propofol, did not keep sufficient medical records and was negligent in his use of medications on Jackson. Murray's civil attorney, Charles Peckham, denied that Murray gave Jackson anything life-threatening

After the death of Jackson the sales of his records increased by almost eighty times the amount of the previous week. In the UK, on the Sunday following his death, his albums occupied 14 of the top 20 places on the Amazon.co.uk sales chart, with 'Off The Wall' at the top. 'Number Ones' reached the top of the UK Album Chart, and his studio albums occupied number two to number eight on the iTunes Music Store top albums. Six of his songs charted in the top 40: 'Man in the Mirror' (11), 'Thriller' (23), 'Billie Jean' (25), 'Smooth Criminal' (28), 'Beat It' (30), and 'Earth Song' (38). The following Sunday, 13 of Jackson's songs charted in the top 40, including 'Man In the Mirror', which landed the number two spot.

According to reports, Jackson's burial was originally scheduled for August 29, 2009 which would have been his 51st birthday. His service and burial was held at Forest Lawn Cemetery of Glendale on September 3, 2009, 10 weeks to the day after his death. The burial was attended by his family members, first wife Lisa Marie Presley as well as his old friends Macaulay Culkin and Elizabeth Taylor, amongst others. The service began with Jackson's three children placing a golden crown on his casket in tribute to his title as the King of Pop. It was estimated that almost a billion people worldwide watched the memorial service.

116 Michael Jackson **THE MAN IN THE MIRROR**